The Needle Arts

TIME-LIFE BOOKS

Alexandria, Virginia

The Needle Arts

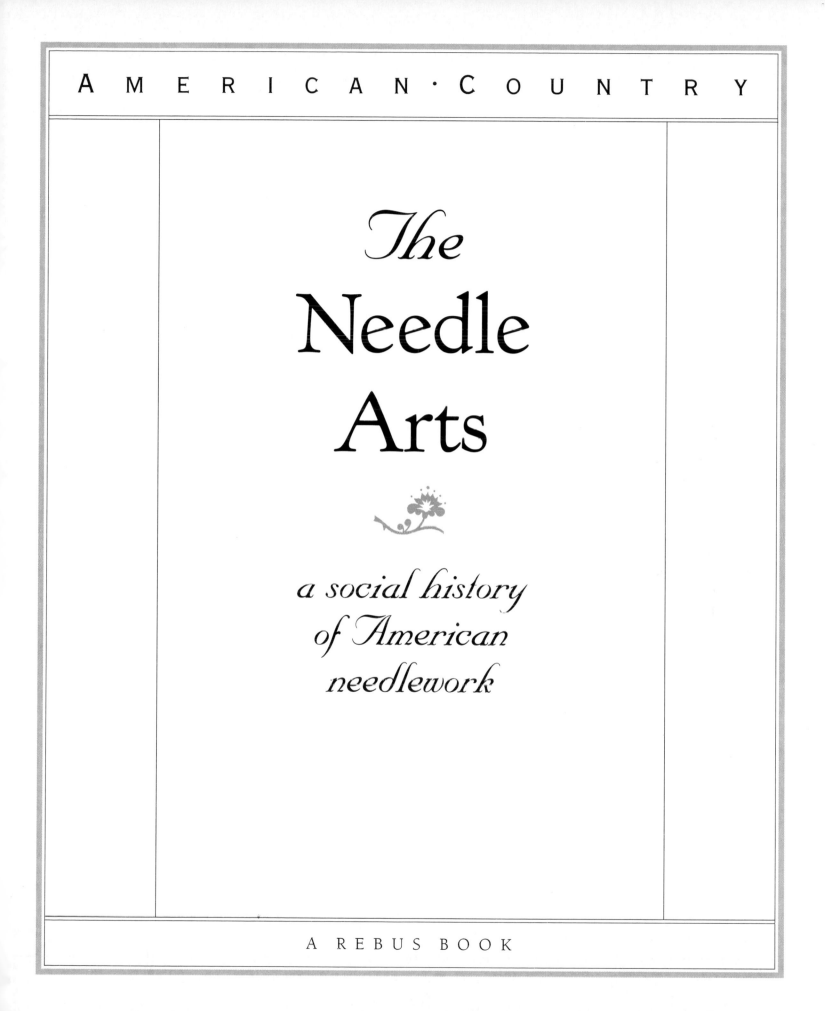

*a social history
of American
needlework*

A REBUS BOOK

CONTENTS

Needlework in the Home

Collecting by Design · A Respect for Fine Stitchery
An Eye for Comfort

144

NEEDLEWORK TECHNIQUES

166

CREDITS

168

INDEX

170

ACKNOWLEDGMENTS

175

The story of American needlework is essentially a woman's story. Nearly all of the stitchery presented in this volume—dating from the 1600s to the early 20th century—is the work of females, and it represents their most important contribution to the American decorative arts during this period. For the most part, it is distinguished by an artistry equal to that of other contemporary handcrafts, such as silversmithing and woodworking, that were traditionally in the male domain. A remarkable difference, however, is that stitchery was generally not the handiwork of professionals, but of school-age girls, or of women with homes and families demanding their full attention.

Undertaken along with many other household duties, needlework was an ever-present part of daily life, and it was advantageous to be good at it. Until the mid-19th century, in fact, a girl's skill with the needle symbolized her eligibility for marriage, and, once she was wed, it remained a measure of her success and value as a housewife. "Needle-work, in all its forms of use, elegance and ornament, has ever been the appropriate occupation of woman...," wrote Lydia Sigourney in her 1837 volume *Letters to Young Ladies*, "... it has been both their duty and their resource."

Those for whom needlework was primarily a "duty" often had to confine their labors to the plain sewing necessary for making bed and table linens, as well as the family's clothing. In 1889, one Lucy Larcom recalled thinking in her youth, "I suppose I have got to grow up and have a husband, and put all those little stitches into his coats and pantaloons. Oh, I never, never can do it!"

The kind of plain-sewn pieces that Lucy dreaded stitching were used and laundered until they fell apart; as a result, early examples are rare today. What has survived, as shown in this volume, is mostly fancywork: samplers, "best" quilts and coverlets, canvaswork table covers, crewelwork bed hangings, Berlinwork pictures, silk-embroidered tea cloths, and other pieces intended primarily for show.

The women who did such fancywork followed fads originating both in this country and in Europe, and the designs, colors, and stitches they employed were dictated by current fashions. In general, the makers were fortunate enough to have the time and money to spend on handiwork that would ensure a stylish decor. Yet, even beyond fashion, fancy needlework provided females with the important "resource" to which Lydia Sigourney referred: for most women who wielded a needle, it was one of the few available outlets for creativity, and the stitchery that has passed down through the generations constitutes an invaluable record of their artistry and skill. Today, fine needlework is prized not only for the ingenious approaches that the makers took in transforming fabric and thread into beautiful objects, but also for its craftsmanship. The hundreds or even thousands of stitches that went into each piece, and the innumerable hours of labor the finished works required, in themselves represent accomplishments that should not pass unnoticed.

Stitches in Time

*remarkable needlework from
the colonial period to the
Victorian era*

From the colonial era through much of the 1800s in America, almost all females sewed. For a well-to-do individual, "fancy sewing" provided an afternoon's pastime, but her skills in decorative needlework also presented proof that she was well trained in the social graces—and indeed a lady. For a woman in less comfortable circumstances, practical "plain" work was an endless necessity; she made and mended her family's clothing, hemmed and marked the household linens, and knitted mittens and socks.

The styles and techniques of both decorative embroidery and plainwork hold an important place in the history of American needle arts. Some, like lacework, memorial embroidery, and Victorian Berlin work, were passing fashions, while others, such as knitting, remained mainstays throughout the years. Together, they offer a compelling insight into the nature of women's lives during America's first three centuries.

*A detail from a circa 1750 canvaswork picture (page 24) demonstrates the fine
workmanship that was characteristic of tent stitch.*

American Samplers

Before the 19th century, sewing instruction was the only education that many females received. Lessons began in childhood, and the standard teaching tool was the sampler: a piece of cloth (usually linen) on which needlework techniques were practiced. The sampler tradition was brought to this country by settlers in the 17th century. Although embroidery books were then being printed in Europe, they were rare, and samplers provided a more accessible means of recording stitches.

The earliest American samplers were very narrow in shape, measuring up to thirty inches long and eight inches wide. Stylized designs in silk or linen thread were stitched across the fabric background in formal rows; the same motifs and stitches could then be easily copied on a bed sheet or tablecloth. Finely worked, such samplers typically included the decorative eyelet, arrowhead, Montenegrin, and spider web stitches, as well as the versatile cross-stitch.

Little thought was given to the design of such fancywork pieces, since they were not meant for display but were instead kept rolled up in a sewing basket. Used throughout a woman's life, they could be pulled out and consulted when necessary, and perhaps further embellished when new stitches were learned. During the

Continued

Mary Holingworth's circa 1665 fancywork sampler, right, is one of the earliest known pieces made in America. It measures 25 inches long and only 7½ inches wide.

Most young girls worked on "marking samplers" in order to learn useful stitches. The circa 1815 piece above was made by Betsy Crosman, who was raised by the Shakers. Elisabeth Fisher, an Amish girl, used traditional Pennsylvania-German motifs on her 1808 sampler, left.

11

The 1752 Philadelphia lacework piece above was done entirely in cutwork by Rebekah Jones. Frances Paschal of Delaware used two lacework techniques in her 1788 sampler, right. The corner circles and her name are done in cutwork, while the delicate leaves and flower petals show off her skills at drawnwork.

American women began making darning samplers in the 1700s and continued the practice over the course of the next century; the cotton-on-linen piece at left dates to 1873. Its fine workmanship demonstrates how the weaves of twills and other fabrics could be imitated with darning. Colored threads permitted the needleworker to see that her stitches were perfectly aligned.

1700s, samplers became increasingly shorter—and more manageable for young fingers—until by the end of the century they were small rectangles or squares. Within the new format, needleworkers began to combine lettering with decorative borders and motifs, creating artistic compositions designed to be displayed like pictures.

While fancywork samplers continued to be made, more practical types were also done in the 18th century. The most common were "marking samplers," comprising numerals and the letters of the alphabet sewn in cross-stitch. Working on such a sampler allowed a young girl to learn her numbers and letters, and even more important, it enabled her to mark linens and clothing. This was a necessary chore at a time when a family might have as many as fifteen children in it.

Equally useful for teaching an important skill were darning samplers, which also had become popular by the middle of the 1700s. In these samplers, holes were made in a piece of fabric and then "repaired"; the finished works showed off the needleworker's prowess at imitating the variety of fabric weaves that she would no doubt encounter during a lifetime of mending.

Fashionable 18th-century ladies with time at their disposal might try their hand at lacework, which was used to imitate expensive imported trimmings. Thus samplers were also made with lacy designs done in cutwork, a technique in which shapes were cut out of a piece of fine cotton or linen and then filled in with rows and webs of buttonhole stitches. Another method

Continued

Ann Wheeley worked the words, flower motifs, and heart-decorated bands on the linen sampler at right entirely in cross-stitch. Schoolgirl samplers like Ann's piece, done in 1832 when she was eleven, frequently incorporated verses; God, death, and one's reward in heaven were popular subjects.

was drawn-thread work, also known as Dresden work, which involved removing several warp or weft threads from the fabric weave and pulling the remaining threads together with embroidery stitches to form delicate patterns.

Throughout most of the 1700s, decorative and practical needlework were taught at home, but by the end of the century it was possible for more and more children to learn the needle arts in the private schools that were beginning to proliferate. The very young might attend a "dame's school," which was usually run by a sin-

Typical of genealogical samplers, the 1819 silk-on-linen piece at left, by Sophia Dyer, was stitched with the needleworker's family record and a memorial scene. Such embroideries were ongoing projects, and the dates of marriages and deaths were often added in many years after the sampler was begun.

gle woman or widow in her home. Here, both boys and girls learned to sew by working a cross-stitch alphabet sampler, and perhaps studied the rudiments of reading.

For many girls, schooling ended at the dame's school. With their knowledge of basic sewing, females could be more useful at home, especially if finances were limited. When family circumstances demanded, some girls were indentured as housekeepers or seamstresses in wealthy households in return for room and board. The hope was that at the end of her service, a young wom-

Continued

15

The 1799 sampler above represents the family record of Leah Galligher and Rachel Armstrong, twin sisters who ran a school in Pennsylvania.

an would have the housewifely skills needed to attract a husband despite her lack of dowry.

If her family was affluent, however, a girl was likely to be sent to a needlework school or to a private young ladies' academy. Here she might stay for a few quarters or for several years (pupils were generally in their teens, but might be as young as ten or as old as thirty). While most academies offered subjects such as French and history, they were essentially finishing schools, and emphasis was placed on dancing, draw-

ing, deportment, and, of course, needlework.

Having already worked an alphabet sampler as a young girl, the academy student was taught to make a fancier type of needlework piece, if she had the talent. These schoolgirl samplers continued to include neat rows of cross-stitched letters, but the compositions, incorporating biblical verses, sentimental poetry, and pictorial borders, were considerably more involved than those of plain alphabet samplers. Many pieces included a record of births, deaths, and mar-

See youth and beauty bloom one transient hour
But age leaves not one flatering trace behind
But there is one charm over which time has no Power
The beauty of a cultivated mind

Haste then dear youth and make this charm thine own
See meek religion Points you out the way
Give her thy hand and She will lead thee on
Where virtue blossms in eternal day

Wrought by Catharine Mary Wheeler in the 13 year of her age Jane Keys Instructress of Brunswick School 1825

riages in the needleworker's family; such genealogical samplers were one of the most popular sampler forms in America, and are thought to have originated in this country.

The designs of schoolgirl samplers, commonly stitched in linen or silk thread on a linen or linsey-woolsey ground, were usually devised by the teacher rather than by the student, and included original creations as well as adaptations of English prototypes. Traditional folk motifs were often worked into the compositions, as were "portraits" of family homes or local landmarks. Because specific stitching styles and imagery became popular in certain parts of the country, samplers from a particular town or school tended to look alike. The stitches varied with the type of picture, but typically included satin, split, Gobelin, and chain stitches, French knots, and couching. Such fancywork would not be useful in plain sewing, but it did show off a girl's ability with a needle. The object of her labors, after all, was to ensure a suitable marriage.

The designs of the house and stepped lawn on the sampler above are typical of pieces from the Delaware River Valley. The two shepherdesses and the sheep were done in silk-embroidered appliqué.

The long, diagonal crinkled-silk stitches used to fill in the background of the sampler above are characteristic of pieces made at Sarah Stivour's school in Salem, Massachusetts. The crinkling, which occurred when embroidery thread was unraveled, was favored for its especially shiny effect.

Samplers done on a colored ground, like the piece above, by Beulah Purinton of Massachusetts, are rare.

Beulah worked her design in French knots and satin, whip, and eyelet stitches, using crinkled silk.

As is common, the script alphabet is missing the letters I and U.

PRACTICAL POCKETS

Anyone who remembers the nursery rhyme in which "Lucy Locket lost her pocket" may also recall wondering how she did it. In fact, in Lucy's day, misplacing a pocket was not at all improbable, for, until the 1840s, pockets were not sewn into clothing but were worn separately. A woman would tie her pockets (generally made in pairs) by a string around her waist, placing them under her skirt and over her petticoat. Sometimes measuring as long as fifteen inches, generously sized pockets like the antique pieces at right might be used to hold sewing or knitting projects; slits in the side seams of the wearer's skirt provided access to the contents.

Although the pockets were not usually visible, they could be surprisingly decorative, and might be elaborately embroidered. Such fancywork pockets were often made by young ladies to be part of their trousseaux, or were stitched as gifts. Making pockets was also an ideal project for a child learning to sew. At her mother's knee a little girl could stitch her first patchwork, seams, and bindings, ending up with her own colorful carryalls.

Early Canvaswork

Canvaswork pictures made in the mid-18th century were apt to show well-dressed ladies and gentlemen engaged in fashionable pastimes. Among the figures depicted in the tent-stitched piece at right, worked in wool and silk on a linen canvas, is a couple seated at a gaming table.

Magnificent craftsmanship was greatly admired by Americans in the 1700s, and it is not surprising that much of the finest needlework ever stitched in this country dates from that century. Among the most distinctive of all the needle arts fashionable at the time was canvaswork—now known as needlepoint—a type of embroidery worked on an open-weave canvas mesh usually made of linen or hemp. Done throughout the colonies, most early canvaswork pieces were the handiwork of academy students and women of means, since such complex embroidery was out of the ques-

tion for anyone who had cooking, mending, and a houseful of children to attend to.

Stitched over the entire surface of the canvas, early canvaswork was generally done in silk floss or crewel—a two-ply, loosely twisted worsted wool yarn—in tent, queen, and Irish stitches. The tent stitch was simple but tedious to execute because each stitch covered only one thread of the canvas mesh, which was typically very finely woven—as tight as fifty-two threads per inch. (The finest needlepoint canvas used today has only twenty-four threads per inch.) Such painstaking work is particularly remarkable, considering the poor lighting conditions of the time.

Because the tight, tiny tent stitches produced finer detail than any other canvaswork stitch, they were favored for the intricate scenic and floral pictures popular in the 18th century. The effects that could be achieved in a tent-stitched picture were so rich, in fact, that such canvaswork was thought to resemble European tapestries, and the technique was sometimes called tapestrywork. Tent-stitched compositions were generally made by advanced students at the few ladies' academies that existed in the mid-1700s. Requiring a year or more to execute, the projects were probably completed as graduation pieces and taken home to be framed and displayed.

Among the most famous tent-stitched scenes are those referred to as the Fishing Lady pictures (overleaf). Made in Boston at mid-century, about sixty of these pieces are now known to exist. Although they differ in size and composition, the works share common pictorial elements. They are usually pastoral scenes; some feature a beautifully dressed lady angler—fishing was a popular pastime for courting couples in the 18th century—others a reclining shepherdess. The pieces are thought to have been

Continued

The fanciful canvaswork picture above was done by Mary Whitehead around 1750. Often, no attempt was made to achieve realistic perspective in such tent-stitched designs; flowers could be the size of people, and birds the size of buildings.

PRUDENCE PUNDERSON

Prudence Punderson's c. 1775 embroidery above is housed in the Connecticut Historical Society along with many of the furnishings depicted.

Few American needlework pictures of the 18th century reveal as much about the women who made them as those of Prudence Punderson. Born in Preston, Connecticut, in 1758, Punderson studied embroidery as a girl and became a true artist with her needle; her work is notable both for its quality and for the many delightful details she borrowed from the world around her.

Prudence Punderson's best-known embroidery, a depiction of life's passing entitled "The First, Second, and Last Scene of Mortality," was worked when she was about sixteen. The piece is remarkable for its candid glimpse of her family's parlor, a stylish room furnished with Chippendale chairs, a patterned carpet, and a framed needlework picture. The subject for "life's passing" is Punderson herself, portrayed as an infant with her nanny, as a young and well-dressed woman—at work on a piece of embroidery—and, finally, nailed into a coffin marked with her initials. (The gilded mirror hanging behind the coffin is shrouded in linen, following a mourning custom of the day.) It turned out that Punderson's own life was, in fact, quite brief, ending when she was only twenty-six years old.

Less poignant than her parlor scene, yet equally original, is a set of individual portraits depicting the twelve Apostles, stitched by Punderson between 1776 and 1780. The spiritual subjects are definitely of this world; the barefoot Saint Peter, for instance, wears an American tricorn hat and is seated in a Queen Anne chair, while Saint Simon clutches a saw. Punderson's choice of a religious theme for her series of portraits was not unusual for the 18th century, but the freshness and imagination she brought to her remarkable needlework designs were very much her own.

The four needlework portraits above are from Prudence Punderson's series of the twelve Apostles. Clockwise from top left, they include Saint Peter, Judas Iscariot, Saint Simon the Zealot, and Saint John the Evangelist. Like all of Punderson's known needlework pictures, they were worked in silk on a silk-satin background.

Silkwork Pictures

While the trees of the circa 1820 piece above were stitched in silk, the rest of the picture was done in watercolor; the two mediums were often combined in early-19th-century schoolgirl pieces.

Embroidered pictures worked in silk on a silk-satin ground first became fashionable in this country in the mid-1700s. Because silk had to be imported from Europe at that time, the early pieces were extremely costly to undertake. After the Revolution was over, however, America began trading directly with China, and the price of the materials dropped. By around 1800, a fad for silkwork caught on in England, and the technique immediately became extremely popular among American academy students, remaining so through the 1820s.

While the earlier silkwork pictures were more closely related to samplers, the 19th-century pieces were conceived almost as silk paintings, and their makers—who might labor on a piece during the course of several school terms—considered themselves to be true artists.

Ye stubborn oaks, and stately pines, Ye birds, his praise must be your theme, Ye flow'ry plains, proclaim his skill;
Bend your high branches and adore Who form'd to song your tuneful voice; Ye vallies, sink before his eyes
Praise God, ye beasts in different strains While the dumb fish that cuts the stream And let his praise from every hill,
The lamb must bleat the oxen roar, In his protecting care rejoice. Rise tune ful to the neighb'ring skies.

MARY REES 1827 E. Robinson Teacher

The scenes academy pupils chose to stitch in the 1800s also differed in that they reflected the changes beginning to take place in female education. Along with needlework and other "accomplishments," genteel young ladies were now expected to improve their minds. They read novels, studied religion and literature, and analyzed the classical civilizations whose democratic ideals were the models for America's new repub-

lic. Often working from English print sources, girls stitched biblical and literary scenes to show off their knowledge. Characters in their pictures might be dressed in classical garb, and the compositions were apt to include marble temples and perhaps a few verses of lofty poetry expressing the popular themes of love, heroism, and virtue.

These themes and imagery found their full

Continued

Mary Rees stitched the bucolic pastoral scene above on linen, using silk for all of the embroidery except for the sheep's coats, which were done in wool. Her teacher's name also appears.

Beautifully worked in silk,
the memorial embroideries
above and at right show
scrupulous attention to
detail; even the stone in the
plinths was stitched to
resemble veined marble. The
Burgess piece also records
detailed tomb inscriptions for
the needleworker's mother
and two brothers.

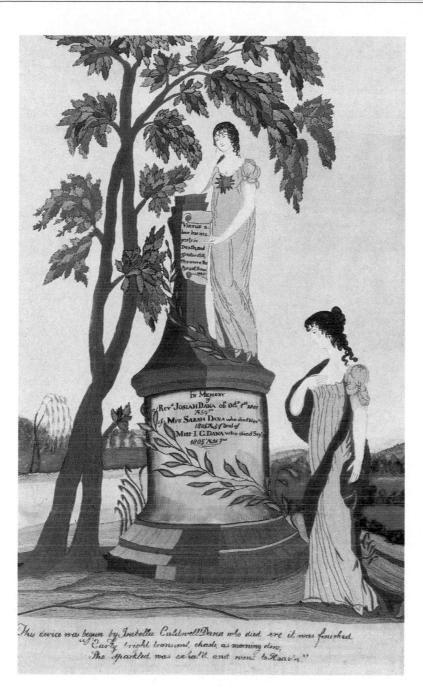

flowering in the vogue for memorial embroideries, which lasted from the late 18th century until the 1830s. Typically featuring elaborate plinths and tombstones, weeping willows, and tearful mourners, these romanticized compositions were all too often stitched by girls following the loss of family members. Many needlework pieces were also made to commemorate George Washington, whose death in 1799 had

an enormous emotional impact on the nation.

As somber as their subject matter was, however, memorial pictures were considered to be stylish home furnishings rather than the morbid mementos they seem today. Worked in silk, chenille, and sparkling metallic threads, the pictures were proudly displayed, appealing as much to the current taste for the classical and antique as to the fashion for sentimentality.

Memorials were often true expressions of grief. Fifteen-year-old Isabella Dana began the picture at left around 1804, in memory of her father, Josiah. After Isabella died in 1805 her bereaved sister, Sarah, continued the piece. Before the work was finished, however, it was necessary to add the name of her mother, who died two months after Isabella.

33

Fancywork from "Godey's"

Basket decorated with crystal beads

Knitted baby's shoe and sock

Hanging pincushion and needlebook

Beginning in the 1830s, innumerable fads for decorative embroidery developed in America and were pursued with widespread enthusiasm by the many middle-class ladies who now had leisure time on their hands. In large part, the interest in needlework novelties was kindled by a wholly new phenomenon: women's magazines. There were several such publications, including *Graham's* and *Peterson's,* but the most popular was *Godey's Lady's Book,* which was founded in 1830 by Louis A. Godey, and edited from 1837 to 1877 by Sarah Josepha Hale— one of America's first female editors.

Establishing a format that is still followed by many women's magazines today, *Godey's* was a compendium of contemporary fiction and articles on health, gardening, women's education, child rearing, and fashion. Each issue also included instructions for fancywork crafts, accompanied by engraved illustrations like those at right. Patterns for Berlin work appeared, as well as many other suggestions for projects involving popular techniques such as beadwork, knitting, crocheting, and punched-paper work.

Slipper watch stand

Beaded napkin ring

Punched-paper watch pocket

Knitted reticule

Berlin-work button case

Punched-paper sewing basket

Beaded butterfly penwipe

Knitted baby's glove

Crocheted knitting bag

Victorian Berlin Work

As public schools became more prevalent in the 1830s, the emphasis in women's education shifted from "accomplishments" to the basics of reading, writing, and arithmetic. Some girls still learned sewing in school, but concentrated on plainwork rather than fancywork. Other girls grew up without ever working a sampler at all. Yet, while females were no longer concerned with mastering intricate embroidery, they remained interested in needlework as a pleasurable pastime. That interest was reflected by the rage for a type of canvaswork called Berlin-wool work, or simply Berlin work, by far the most popular type of stitchery done between the 1830s and 1870s.

Berlin work was easier to do than earlier canvaswork because it was stitched with the help of patterns (first printed in Berlin, Germany) that eliminated any need for conceiving a design, determining shading, or choosing colors. Moreover, most such work was done with German merino wool yarns, known as Berlin wool. Softer and thicker than the crewel yarns used for early canvaswork, Berlin wool was worked on a relatively open-mesh canvas—about twenty-four threads to the inch—which made projects move along quickly. Since entire Berlin-work designs were often done with a single type of stitch (usually tent, cross, or Irish) virtually any woman could become adept at the craft. Best of all, however, Berlin work was versatile. It could be, and was, used for the wide range of projects—including carpet slippers, sentimental pictures, pincushions, ottomans, lambrequins, and bell-pulls—favored during the Victorian period.

Berlin-work patterns could be used with a variety of materials. The circa 1845 still-life design, top, was stitched in wool and silk on a linen background. The picture at bottom, which dates to around 1840, is worked in silk on silk mesh.

Victorian lambrequins, or valances, were used across the tops of windows and interior doorways, and also as shelf trims. The paisley and leaf Berlin-work design, top, was done in tent stitch, the flame design, center, in Irish stitch, and the abstract floral design, bottom, in cross-stitch.

Entitled "Family Happiness," the picture above was one of many popular mid-19th-century Berlin-work designs that featured sentimental scenes of family life.

German publishers catered to American tastes by devising Berlin-work patterns that pictured well-loved

national heroes such as Ben Franklin, who is depicted in the mid-19th-century piece above.

PETERSON'S MAGAZINE, DECEMBER, 1866.

BERLIN WORK PATTERN.

For Sofa Pillow, Footstool, Bag, Ottoman, or Fender-Stool, &c. &c.

Charity for All.

Malice toward None

FOR THE LADIES

BERLIN-WORK PATTERNS

Early in the 19th century, German printers in Berlin devised a means of mapping out canvaswork designs on a type of graph, or "point," paper. On black-and-white patterns, the squares of the graph were marked with tiny symbols indicating what shade of wool was to be used. Colored patterns—at first hand-painted, and eventually printed—were also available. The needleworker followed the patterns simply by counting squares on the graph and stitching in the appropriate colors on the canvas. It was even easier to use patterns for punched-paper work—a Berlin-work variation that appeared in the 1870s—as these were printed right onto the perforated cards that were to be stitched.

Imported Berlin-work patterns were used in America to a limited extent until the 1840s, when women's periodicals began including reproductions of the patterns and suggestions for copying them; patterns were also available in "fancy shops." Publishers in Vienna and Paris soon followed Germany's lead in devising designs, and thousands were produced. They ranged from geometric and floral patterns—used for such furnishings and accessories as footstools, sofa pillows, pincushions, and tea cozies—to scenes that could be framed and displayed as pictorial "art." Over time, the designs became increasingly sentimental and ornate in response to Victorian tastes.

Plushwork

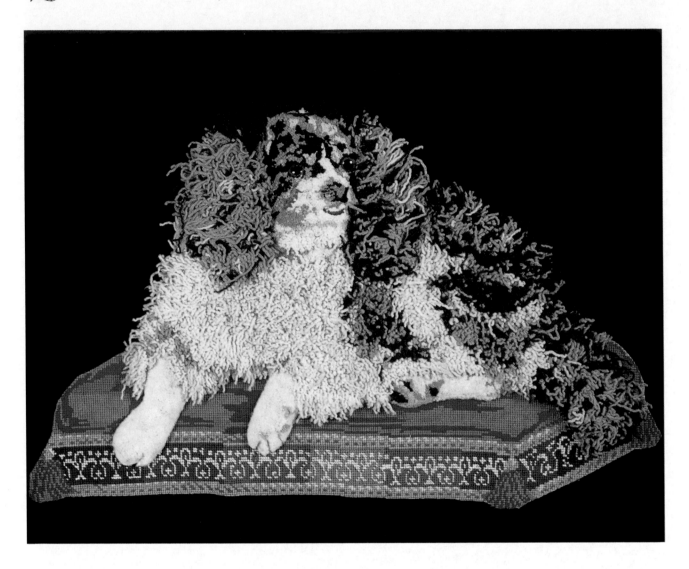

The King Charles spaniel, the particular breed owned by Queen Victoria, became a popular subject in 19th-century needlework. In the picture above, the dog's coat, face, and paws were executed in plushwork, a variation on the Berlin-work technique.

For the most part, Victorian house interiors leaned toward decorative excess. In an era when no surface was left uncovered, middle-class women were always on the lookout for projects that would keep their hands busy and add that extra exotic, colorful, or sentimental touch to their rooms. If nothing else, the abundance of household embellishments that women managed to turn out during the Victorian period represented the virtues of industriousness and a tireless devotion to feathering the family nest.

As the taste for novelty increased, several variations on Berlin work developed that could be made using the same patterns. Among these was plushwork, which was characterized by raised stitches (like those on hooked rugs) that formed a napped surface. Left untrimmed, the stitches created a long, loopy effect; cropped close, they yielded a soft, fuzzy surface. If the needleworker desired, she could appliqué a plushwork design to a solid-colored fabric; this eliminated the laborious task of filling in the background of a piece with stitching.

*The maker of the table cover above stitched the plushwork hunting scene and corner designs
directly onto a wool background. The floral border is done in Berlin work.*

*These late-19th-century punched-paper pictures show similar houses, with imaginative variations
on the theme. Bits of lace and fabric were worked into the piece at top, while the design at
bottom is embellished with lithographed paper cutouts.*

Many of the most popular punched-paper patterns sold in the late 19th century featured homely sayings or blessings like those stitched into the pictures at left. Often done in variegated wools, such pieces were customarily framed and hung over doorways.

Purls of Wisdom

While it was not essential for the woman in Victorian America to knit in order to keep her family in warm clothing—as it had been for her colonial counterpart—the Puritan work ethic continued to dictate that her hands be busy during her waking hours. Lest she forget this, ladies' magazines and books of the period bombarded her with the message that, in order to be a good wife, she had to be forever making things to beautify her home. The 1894 edition of *Dainty Work for Pleasure and Profit,* for example, made it clear that a diligent homemaker should use her "nimble fingers" to create "accessories in the shape of mantel drapes, screens, wall-pockets, toilet sets, dainty table linen, cushions, photograph holders, and all the numberless odds and ends that go to make up the pretty home . . . ."

There were other, cautionary lessons to be heeded as well. An 1887 book entitled *Knitting and Crochet: A Guide to the Use of the Needle and the Hook* counseled knitters that, when young, their skill with the needles might be "a defense against weariness," but that by the time they reached middle age, "that terrible period to women, when they have lost the charm of youth, without acquiring the veneration due to age," knitting would be a way to "lighten their monotonous hours . . . ."

Women's publications further suggested that homemakers knit while engaged in other activities, such as reading or nursing a baby. In 1848, *A Winter Gift for Ladies* proposed that women knit "when passing a morning visit, or after dinner at a dinner party, or while sipping coffee, or taking ices at the public gardens . . . ."

And although such needlework treatises also proclaimed knitting to be "the friend of the aged and blind," and a skill that even the "most stupid" could practice, the instructions they offered were generally so complicated as to baffle the most astute knitter. The *Ladies' Guide to Needlework,* published in 1877, acknowledged this by commenting that if two different women used the same yarn and the same needles to make a tidy, "one would produce a square hardly large enough to cover a pincushion, while the work of the other could be used for a bed-spread."

Knitting

Knitting is one of the earliest, most practical, and longest-lasting of all the needle arts in America. During the colonial period, children were taught to knit by the time they were six years old. Even though the colonies imported knitted goods from England, there was a never-ending need for more warm mittens and caps in the winter, and stockings all year round. (Colonial men traditionally wore white stockings, but females wore colorful versions under their long skirts.)

Some colonial women—and men too—earned an income by knitting professionally. More often, however, wives and daughters produced the knitted goods used by their families. Warm clothing was knitted from wool, while more personal articles such as decorative little handbags —usually the province of delicate ladies—were traditionally worked in silk.

Fortunately, knitting was not the most arduous of chores. It was easily picked up and put down, and could be carried from one place to another. Since knitting left the mind free while keeping the hands busy, women often worked on their projects during visits with their friends over tea, or while listening to their children recite school lessons at home.

Knitting remained popular among the well-to-do until the Civil War, for making such articles as lace, shawls, and throws. But by the turn of the century, the taste for such pieces had faded, and knitting, too, fell from fashion, becoming, for the time being, a pastime mainly of the elderly.

Worked on tiny needles, the small silk handbags above were all knitted by Mary Wright Alsop of Middletown, Connecticut, in the early 19th century.

The Well-Dressed Bed

traditional quilts, spreads, blankets,
and hangings stitched
in America

In the colonial period, when a single room served numerous purposes, the master bed—often the most expensive piece of furniture in a household—was customarily placed in the parlor. There it served as a showpiece, perhaps dressed with a handsome yarn-sewn bed rug, or with a set of crewel-embroidered bed "furniture" that might include an intricately stitched coverlet and several hangings.

By the mid-1700s, the notion of privacy, and of separate rooms for sleeping, had become more widespread, and the bed was no longer such a prominent furnishing. Effort and time, however, were still devoted to stitching beautiful bedcovers—although the more elaborate of these were often put away in dower chests. Included among the remarkable range of pieces produced over the years are embroidered woolen blankets, cotton coverlets, whitework spreads, and of course, the familiar quilts that have become hallmarks of American needlework.

Appliquéd animals, including a pair of ostriches, can be seen in a detail of a
finely stitched 19th-century quilt top (page 83).

Hannah Johnson of Bozrah, Connecticut, stitched the bed rug above in 1796, when she was an unmarried

lady of twenty-six. Such pieces were often made to mark special occasions, and Hannah may have

created this rug in anticipation of her wedding.

After a lifetime of sewing, seventy-one-year-old Rachel Packard from Jericho, Vermont, was certainly

an experienced needlewoman when she stitched the rug above, completed in 1805. The bold

floral motifs resemble those found in 18th-century canvaswork.

By inscribing her name boldly over the stylized vase of flowers on the rug above, Mary Comstock of Shelburne, Vermont, showed she was proud of the piece, which she finished at age sixty-six.

The bed rug above, stitched by Dorothy Seabury of Stowe, Vermont, was worked primarily in browns,
which were relatively easy colors to produce with homemade dyes.

Crewelwork Bed Furniture

In the 17th and 18th centuries, beds in every colonial household of sufficient means were dressed for warmth and privacy with sets of "bed furniture," which might include a coverlet, a headcloth, three or four valances (depending on whether the bed was against the wall), side curtains, a tester cloth (canopy), and bases, attached to the bed rail.

Embroidered bed furniture was probably first made in this country in the 1700s. The various pieces were usually worked on linen or linen-blend backgrounds and stitched with crewel, a loosely twisted, two-ply woolen yarn. While the linen and the yarn were produced domestically, they were also imported from England, where crewelwork developed in the 1500s.

Many of the designs found in American crewelwork—which was used for draperies, upholstery, and clothing as well—also came from abroad, and were copied from pattern books brought to this country by settlers. Even designs originated by American needlework teachers or by the embroiderer herself were influenced by the English penchant for elaborate nature scenes. American pieces differed from their English counterparts, however, in their simplicity and economy; a minimum of yarn was used and the stitches were simpler.

Measuring 64 by 77 inches, the crewel-embroidered linen bed curtain at left was made in the early 1700s near Boston. Incorporating a tree of life motif, the design features fantastical plants and naturalistic animals, and is expertly executed: different colored yarns provide shading, while a variety of stitches give textural contrast.

The valances are stitched with poignant verses from a pastoral poem.

The flowering trees and flower baskets depicted on the headcloth were common crewel motifs.

These two narrow panels hang by the head of the bed, one on either side.

This curtain, with the one at right, is used at the foot of the bed.

Shaped to fit a particular bed frame, the coverlet features borders of vines.

This foot curtain is similar, but not identical, to its mate at left.

THE BULMAN BED FURNITURE

Sometime around 1745, Mary Bulman of York, Maine, began embroidering a set of bed furniture. Her handwork, which includes a coverlet, headcloth, three valances, and four curtains—now displayed on the bed above, at the Old York Historical Society—is the only complete set of American wool-on-linen bedclothes to survive from the 1700s.

Mary's talent with the needle was remarkable. Her exquisite crewelwork coverlet and hangings feature an original design incorporating graceful floral sprays, delicate trees, vines, and birds. Especially notable are the valances, with their finely worked verses taken from the 1706 poem "Meditation in a Grove."

Mary probably began her stitching to occupy her time while her husband served in a campaign against the French in Canada. He died, but her work continued for seven years —through her widowhood and into her second marriage.

Embroidered Blankets

The maker of the circa 1770 embroidered blanket at right devised an imaginative twist on a common theme. Rather than using one flower basket as a central design, she arranged five different baskets along the edges and let the floral sprays spread in profusion over the background.

Almost every colonial household owned at least one wool blanket—sometimes several—and embroidering these textiles was a common occupation by the late 1700s. Becoming popular at a time when making bed rugs and crewelwork hangings was falling from fashion, the practice remained relatively widespread, especially in the more rural areas, into the mid-19th century.

The blankets themselves might be purchased from a professional weaver or made at home. Since the fabrics were produced in widths of no more than thirty-six inches—which was approximately the distance a weaver could throw the shuttle on a hand loom—it was necessary to seam together two or more of these narrow panels to yield a whole bedcover. The wool was generally woven in a solid color or in a plaid

The elegantly worked blanket at left, made in New England in the late 18th century, displays designs closely resembling those found on the crewelwork coverlets that were then fading from fashion. The central floral spray was adapted from the tree of life motif, commonly used in needlework of the period.

pattern; either could serve as an effective background for the embroidered designs.

Often homespun, the yarns were dyed primarily in blues and browns. A wide range of stitches were used, from the simple to the elaborate, but favorite choices included the relatively easy-to-work running and outline stitches. Usually, the decorative needlework on a plain blanket—which might be dyed a dark tint with vegetable colors or left a natural cream-white—ranged across its entire surface. On plaid blankets, which were most frequently white with blue lines, the embroidery was confined within the pattern of squares and often comprised small floral or geometric motifs. A central square or the top border might be reserved for an inscription, such as the date the piece was completed or the maker's name or initials.

The linen candlewick spread above was made in 1825 in Connecticut. The weeping willow was a symbol of mourning.

As a taste for a light, classical look in furnishings developed in the early 19th century, elegant white bedcovers became fashionable. Embroidered with white yarn or thread on a white linen or cotton background, these spreads were found primarily in well-to-do households.

Because color did not enter into the basic design of a whitework spread, texture and shape alone defined the surface pattern, which was slightly raised. This sculptural effect could be achieved with different techniques, among them candlewicking and stuffedwork. The first involved embroidering one layer of cloth with thick cotton thread or yarn that resembled the cord used for candlewicks. The yarn or thread

Whitework Spreads

Appliquéd flowers were used to accent the padded designs on the circa 1850 stuffedwork spread at left. The nautical motifs, including two skillfully wrought clipper ships framed in raised medallions, might signify that the maker lived in a port town.

could be drawn through the fabric to create loops or fringe, or stitched directly onto the fabric to form solid lines. Stuffedwork required a finely woven top and a coarser backing, which were sewn together with decorative needlework. Some of the stitches outlined motifs and created "channels" for padding material, which would be forced bit by bit through small openings made between the threads of the backing. Once the piece was washed, the holes would close up.

Whitework spreads often featured the classical or patriotic symbols fashionable at the time, including urns, grape clusters, swags, cornucopia, and eagles, as well as the traditional floral and star motifs. The most intricate designs could take years to complete.

CRAZYWORK DECOR

In 1884, the editor of *Dorcas Magazine* asserted that "of all the 'crazes' which have swept over and fairly engulfed some of us, there is none which has taken a deeper hold upon the fair women of our land than this one of crazy patchwork."

Lasting from the 1876 Centennial to around 1900, the intense fad for stitching bits of silk and velvet into kaleidoscopic patterns for quilts and accessories came at a time when the Victorian woman was expected to make her home an oasis in an "ugly" world. Ideally, she was to do so by creating an "artistic" environment with her handcrafts, and crazywork proved perfect for the task. The random mix of fabrics characteristic of this patchwork ensured an original look—necessary in "true art"—while the decorative stitching that was worked on such pieces offered the opportunity for suitably elaborate needlework. The striking, asymmetrical patterns, influenced by Japanese design, also satisfied a contemporary taste for the exotic.

As the craftsmanship involved in crazywork was extremely intricate and time consuming, the makers were naturally eager to show off their pieces. Thus, crazywork quilts made the move from bedroom to parlor, where they might be draped over a day bed or piano—in plain view for all to admire. And for those who could not make a large piece, a crazywork chair tidy, table scarf, or ottoman cover would do just as well to embellish a room in proper style.

THE DEERFIELD SOCIETY OF BLUE AND WHITE NEEDLEWORK

In 1898, when Ellen Miller and Margaret Whiting, artists who lived in Deerfield, Massachusetts, discovered some 18th-century pieces of crewel embroidery in the town museum, crewelwork had long been out of fashion. At a time when most needlework was done with commercial patterns and materials, the women were extremely impressed by the high quality and originality of the early embroideries. Inspired, they set out to create a record of the deteriorating museum pieces, teaching themselves the stitches that the colonial needleworkers had used, and assembling a portfolio of patterns adapted from early works.

As their own knowledge and needle skills advanced, the two artists found that people were interested not only in buying their work, but also in learning how to do the stitching themselves. Thus, the Deerfield Society of Blue and White Needlework was born; under a cooperative arrangement, Miller and Whiting provided training to the members—who would eventually number about thirty—while allowing them to share in the revenues from the sale of the embroidered doilies, table mats, and other household linens they stitched. Among the first associated groups of craft workers in America, the Society clearly embraced the philosophy of the current Arts and Crafts movement, which advocated a profitable revival of the "honest" handcraftsmanship that had been eclipsed in an industrial age.

In this vein, Society members rejected commercially manufactured materials in favor of those that were handmade. Homespun thread, and

Members of the Deerfield Society of Blue and White Needlework crafting an embroidered coverlet; c. 1900

handwoven linen fabric for the embroidery backgrounds, were purchased, while Miller and Whiting personally produced natural dyes. Even the Society insignia, a "D" inside a spinning wheel, emphasized handcraftsmanship.

Based on some of the museum pieces, the early embroideries stitched by Miller and Whiting were done in indigo-dyed blue thread on natural linen backgrounds (inspiring the name of the Society), but other colors were introduced almost immediately. Not intended as replicas, the new works showed many departures from 18th-century crewelwork traditions. Notably, Society pieces were done in linen thread rather than the less durable wool that their predecessors had used. Also, as artists, Miller and Whiting were quite interested in creating original work of their own. As well as producing historically based designs, they devised many new patterns, a number of which reflected the current vogue for art nouveau. Even their stitches were not always traditional; Deerfield Society pieces, for example, were frequently done in cross-stitch, which was not typical of colonial embroidery.

Embraced by the Deerfield community, where a number of artists lived, the Deerfield Society prospered for thirty years. Its work was exhibited to acclaim, and drew crowds of buyers. During the First World War, however, output decreased as the women turned their energies to rolling bandages and knitting socks to help the war effort. As interest in the needlework waned after the war, there were fewer orders, and in 1926 the aging founders regretfully disbanded the Society.

A cross-stitch pattern, a departure
from early crewelwork designs; c. 1905

An art nouveau dragonfly pattern
worked on blue-dyed linen; c. 1910

A satin stitch design, seldom found in
Deerfield pieces; c. 1900

A traditional 18th-century embroidery design stitched in blue and white; c. 1900

A stylized floral design adapted from
an 18th-century embroidery; 1890s

Art nouveau poppies in herringbone,
feather, and outline stitches; 1899

Geometric motifs are much rarer than pictorial themes on yarn-sewn floor coverings. The rugs above, found in southern Maine, were probably the work of the same maker and feature vibrantly colored squares, circles, and diamonds.

CARE OF ANTIQUE RUGS

More fragile than many antiques, old rugs require special care to preserve their easily damaged fibers. If shopping for a rug, buy one that is in good condition, without stains. When squeezed lightly, the textile should feel supple, not dry; a rug that is dried out will be brittle and may shed powdery flakes, caused by the breakdown of the backing.

Professional conservators should be consulted about major restoration problems, but general care of a rug in good condition can be undertaken at home. Never shake or beat an antique rug or put it in a washing machine, as such treatment can damage the backing and dislodge fibers. To clean the rug, sweep it lightly with a soft brush. Vacuuming the top—but not the backing—is also acceptable for removing loose dirt, so long as the rug is protected with a clean piece of fiber-glass screening.

If a rug requires washing and can withstand it, the textile should first be tested for colorfastness by wetting a small area with a little cold water. Blot the area with a white cloth; if the dye does not bleed onto the cloth, the fibers should be colorfast. Next, dip a sponge in cold water mixed with mild detergent and squeeze it almost dry. To clean the rug, dab or gently rub the surface with the sponge in a circular motion, then rinse by sponging with cold water; avoid wetting the backing.

As a last resort, a heavily soiled rug can be soaked. Use cold, soapy water, and leave the rug immersed no longer than one hour. Loosen the dirt with a sponge or brush, but do not agitate the rug; rinse the piece well in cold water. Take special care when handling a wet rug: the added weight of the water can cause the piece to tear if it is not supported properly. Do not wring or squeeze a wet rug, or hang one on a line. Instead, blot the rug by rolling it in a towel with the front side out. Unroll the rug, then lay it flat, turning it over periodically as it dries.

An antique rug should not be exposed to excessive wear or direct sun. To protect the backing, place a synthetic-fiber pad beneath the piece. If storing the rug, do not fold it; lay it flat or roll it loosely, front side out. Keep it in a sheet or towel—never in a plastic bag—in a clean, dark, dry place where the temperature remains around 70 degrees.

THE RUGS OF EDWARD FROST

The finished rugs, right, show two variations on the catalog drawing above. The rugmakers used different colored fabrics, changing the design slightly to suit their own tastes.

One evening in 1868, Edward Sands Frost, a tin peddler and machinist from Maine, noticed a new needlework project his wife had begun: she was hooking a rug. Intrigued, Frost sat down to help with the task himself, and by the time the piece was finished he had decided that he could improve on the design. His supposition was indeed correct, and within two years he had stopped peddling tin and become the country's first commercial producer of hooked rug patterns, maintaining a shop in Biddeford, Maine, and a branch office in Boston at a store by the name of Gibbs & Warren.

Frost's earliest designs, peddled door to door from his cart, were hand-drawn. Orders came in so fast, however, that the entrepreneur soon turned to stenciling as a means of mass-production, cutting his first templates from scrap tin in his stable. Eventually, Frost had some 750 templates, most made of zinc, that were used in various combinations to stencil more than 180 different designs in color onto burlap backgrounds; the pieces to be made ranged from chair seats to rugs measuring nine feet long.

While some of the Frost designs were original, many were copied or adapted from finished rugs that Frost acquired, through barter or purchase, on his travels along the back roads of Maine. The majority displayed floral or animal themes, but patriotic and Masonic symbols, and a variety of geometric motifs, also appeared; among his most unusual patterns were a group imitating imported Oriental rugs.

Frost retired in 1876, selling his business to James A. Strout, who continued to produce the rug patterns until 1900 under the name E. S. Frost & Co. It was probably Strout who recorded the designs in the illustrated catalogs that started to become available at about this time; it is thought that shops kept such catalogs on hand so that needleworkers could choose their patterns from the numbered designs.

The catalog drawing, near right, shows a reclining spaniel surrounded by a floral wreath; the needleworker who hooked the finished rug, far right, added a braided border of her own design.

By using various stencils, Frost was able to produce elaborate colored patterns on burlap backings like the one at left. The maker hooked directly over the pattern, filling in with her own fabric scraps.

The Lion and Palm design, shown in the catalog drawing far left, was one of Frost's most popular. The maker of the rug at left faithfully followed the design, but chose to work a simpler border.

Known as the Caswell carpet, the embroidered rug above was the ambitious
undertaking of Vermont needleworker Zeruah Higley Guernsey Caswell.
Measuring some 162 square feet and dated 1835, it is an original creation.

THE CASWELL CARPET

Zeruah Higley Guernsey was not yet thirty years old when she undertook one of the most remarkable—and one of the few known—embroidered floor coverings to be stitched in early America. Begun around 1832 and marked with the date 1835, Zeruah's room-sized carpet was designed for her father's parlor and measures approximately 13½ by 12 feet; its size alone is a testament

to the monumental task the piece represents.

Few of Zeruah's contemporaries would have been willing to commit themselves to the work required for such an ambitious project. Moreover, at the time the needleworker made her carpet, householders who could afford them were purchasing manufactured floral-patterned carpets from England and France. Perhaps Zeruah's embroidered rug was her own homemade version of one she could not buy.

Although Zeruah, who lived in the small town of Castleton in northern Vermont, enlisted the help of others in her project, she herself participated in every step of its production. Her own sheep, given to her for the purpose, provided the wool, which

was spun, dyed, and woven at home.

Made up of individual sections—seventy-seven in all—the piece is composed in much the same way an album quilt would be. Each block, of twill-weave wool, was embroidered in chain stitch with a different design. Most of the precise, stylized patterns are variations on floral themes, including flower-filled urns and sprays of blossoms. There are also birds, as well as hearts, a shell, and a butterfly. At the top edge of the carpet, Zeruah added her monogram above six blue blossoms; under the leaves of the plant are stitched "LFM." A block near the right edge is marked "By FB." These last two sets

of initials are thought to be those of two young Potawatomi Indians who studied at the local medical college and boarded in town; the students

apparently worked on the rug, each contributing a design.

Especially notable among the different blocks are three that depict household pets, all of which are seated on striped rag carpets—the more usual floor coverings of the day. A somewhat mysterious block

features the figures of a man and woman, whose identities remain unknown. The lady and her swain evidently had some private meaning for Zeruah, for the needleworker concealed the block by stitching another panel over it; the design was only discovered years later by a subsequent owner of the carpet. Particularly remarkable for its workmanship is the detachable hearth panel, stitched with a basket of flowers and framed by a red sawtooth border, that would be removed when the fireplace was in use.

Zeruah Guernsey married in 1846, becoming Mrs. Caswell, and set up her new home, where she placed the rug on her parlor floor. Although the room was seldom used, it is said that Mrs. Caswell was always willing to allow callers to view, and inevitably admire, her masterpiece.

Museum, Collection, and Photography Credits

Cover: needlework picture—Carol and Stephen Huber, East Lyme, CT; crewel blanket, Shaker pincushion, Victorian sewing pouch, wooden needlecase, beaded miser's purse, scrimshaw tape measure—collection of Rosalind and Edwin Miller; thimbles, scissors, silver filigree thimble case, silver walnut thimble case—Primrose Lane, Manhasset, NY; Hepplewhite chair and sewing table—Bernard and Dean Levy, Inc., NY/photo by Steven Mays. **Frontispiece**: The Metropolitan Museum of Art, NYC, gift of R. Thornton Wilson, 1943, in memory of Florence Ellsworth Wilson (43.16). **Page 8**: courtesy of the Henry Francis du Pont Winterthur Museum, Winterthur, DE. **Page 10**: courtesy of the Essex Institute, Salem, MA. **Page 11**: (top) photo by Paul Rocheleau; (bottom) reprinted by permission of Good Books, Intercourse, PA. **Page 12**: (top) Atwater Kent Museum, Philadelphia, PA; (bottom) courtesy of the Henry Francis du Pont Winterthur Museum, Winterthur, DE. **Page 13**: collection of Rosalind and Edwin Miller, courtesy of the Allentown Art Museum, Allentown, PA. **Page 14**: Shelburne Museum, Inc., Shelburne, VT/photo by Ken Burris. **Page 15**: The Metropolitan Museum of Art, NYC, bequest of Barbara Schiff Sinauer, 1984 (1984.331.3). **Page 16**: courtesy of the Henry Francis du Pont Winterthur Museum, Winterthur, DE. **Page 17**: Abby Aldrich Rockefeller Folk Art Center, Williamsburg, VA. **Page 18**: courtesy of the Essex Institute, Salem, MA. **Page 19**: courtesy of the Henry Francis du Pont Winterthur Museum, Winterthur, DE. **Pages 20-21**: (top row, left to right) New Haven Colony Historical Society, New Haven, CT; America Hurrah, NYC/photo by Rob Whitcomb; collection of Dr. and Mrs. Donald M. Herr/ photo by Rob Whitcomb; collection of Dr. and Mrs. Donald M. Herr/photo by Rob Whitcomb; (middle row, left to right) courtesy of Stella Rubin/photo by Schecter Lee; collection of Rosemarie Machmer/photo courtesy of Thos. K. Woodard American Antiques & Quilts, NYC; courtesy of Stella

Rubin/photo by Schecter Lee; collection of Dr. and Mrs. Donald M. Herr/photo by Rob Whitcomb; (bottom row, left to right) collection of Dr. and Mrs. Donald M. Herr/ photo by Rob Whitcomb; collection of Kathy Schoemer/photo courtesy of Thos. K. Woodard American Antiques & Quilts, NYC; collection of Kathy Schoemer/photo courtesy of Thos. K. Woodard American Antiques & Quilts, NYC; collection of Dr. and Mrs. Donald M. Herr/photo by Rob Whitcomb. **Page 22**: Museum of Art, Rhode Island School of Design, Providence, RI, gift of Mrs. Jesse H. Metcalf. **Page 23**: courtesy of Lyman Allyn Art Museum, New London, CT/photo by Steven Mays. **Page 24**: (top) courtesy of the Henry Francis du Pont Winterthur Museum, Winterthur, DE; (bottom) courtesy of the Museum of Fine Arts, Boston, Seth K. Sweetser Fund. **Page 25**: (top) collection of the Museum of American Folk Art, NYC, promised anonymous gift; (bottom) Colonial Williamsburg Foundation, Williamsburg, VA. **Page 26**: (left) The Metropolitan Museum of Art, NYC, gift of R. Thornton Wilson, 1943, in memory of Florence Ellsworth Wilson (43.16); (right top) courtesy of the Henry Francis du Pont Winterthur Museum, Winterthur, DE; (right bottom) America Hurrah, NYC. **Page 27**: (both) courtesy of the Henry Francis du Pont Winterthur Museum, Winterthur, DE. **Pages 28, 29**: (all) The Connecticut Historical Society, Hartford, CT. **Page 30**: Old Sturbridge Village, Sturbridge, MA/ photo by Henry E. Peach. **Page 31**: Abby Aldrich Rockefeller Folk Art Center, Williamsburg, VA. **Page 32**: (top) Yale University Art Gallery, New Haven, CT, the Mabel Brady Garvan Collection; (bottom) Abby Aldrich Rockefeller Folk Art Center, Williamsburg, VA. **Page 33**: Abby Aldrich Rockefeller Folk Art Center, Williamsburg, VA. **Page 36**: (top) collection of the Albany Institute of History & Art, Albany, NY, bequest of Miss Louise Stafford Gilder; (bottom) collection of Rosalind and Edwin Miller, photo courtesy of the Allentown Museum, Allentown, PA. **Page 37**: (all)

Shelburne Museum, Inc., Shelburne, VT/ photo by Ken Burris. **Page 38**: collection of Rosalind and Edwin Miller, photo courtesy of the Allentown Museum, Allentown, PA. **Page 39**: New Hampshire Historical Society, Concord, NH. **Page 40**: Schwenkfelder Library, Pennsburg, PA. **Page 41**: collection of Rosalind and Edwin Miller, photo courtesy of the Allentown Art Museum, Allentown, PA. **Pages 42-43**: collection of Rosalind and Edwin Miller/photo by Steven Mays. **Page 44**: collection of Rosalind and Edwin Miller, photo courtesy of the Allentown Art Museum, Allentown, PA. **Page 45**: The Metropolitan Museum of Art, NYC, purchase, 1980, funds from various donors (1980.63). **Pages 46, 47**: (all) collection of Rosalind and Edwin Miller/ photos by Rob Whitcomb. **Page 48**: (top) collection of Rosalind and Edwin Miller/ photo by Steven Mays; (bottom) courtesy of the Schenectady Museum and Planetarium, Schenectady, NY/photo by James N. Boorn. **Page 49**: (all) collection of Rosalind and Edwin Miller/photo by Steven Mays. **Page 50**: Shelburne Museum, Inc., Shelburne, VT/photo by Fred G. Hill. **Page 51**: (top row, left to right) collection of Rosalind and Edwin Miller/photo by Steven Mays; collection of Rosalind and Edwin Miller/photo by Steven Mays; courtesy of Evelyn Haertig/ photo by Schecter Lee; (bottom row, left to right) courtesy of Evelyn Haertig/photo by Schecter Lee; collection of Rosalind and Edwin Miller/photo by Steven Mays; Shelburne Museum, Inc., Shelburne, VT/photo by Ken Burris. **Page 53**: (all) courtesy of the Henry Francis du Pont Winterthur Museum, Winterthur, DE. **Page 54**: (top row, left to right) courtesy of Stella Rubin/photo by Schecter Lee; Philadelphia Museum of Art, Philadelphia, PA, gift of Dr. John Joseph Stoudt; Shelburne Museum, Inc., Shelburne, VT/photo by Ken Burris; (middle row, left to right) courtesy of Jeannine Dobbs/photo by Schecter Lee; Shelburne Museum, Inc., Shelburne, VT/photo by Ken Burris; collection of Rosalind and Edwin Miller/photo by Steven Mays; (bottom row, left to right) reprinted by permission of Good Books, Intercourse, PA; courtesy of David Pottinger; reprinted by permission of Good Books, Intercourse, PA. **Page 55**: (top row, all) courtesy of Stella Rubin/photo by Schecter Lee; (bottom row, left to right) reprinted by permission of Good Books, Intercourse, PA; courtesy of David Pottinger; courtesy of David Pottinger. **Page 56**: collection of the Museum of American Folk Art, NYC, gift of the Trustees of the Museum of American Folk Art (1979.7.1). **Page 58**: courtesy of the Wenham Historical Association and Museum, Inc., Wenham, MA. **Page 59**: Yale University Art Gallery, New Haven, CT, the Mabel Brady Garvan Collection. **Page 60**: courtesy of the Art Institute of Chicago, Chicago, IL, gift of the Needlework and Textile Guild of Chicago (1944.27). **Page 61**: from the collections of Henry Ford Museum & Greenfield Village, Dearborn, MI (24-B-145). **Pages 62, 63**: Shelburne Museum, Inc., Shelburne, VT/ photos by Ken Burris. **Pages 64-65**: courtesy of Cora Ginsburg, Inc., NYC/photo by Steven Mays. **Pages 66, 67**: (all) Old York Historical Society, York, Maine. **Page 68**: from the collections of Henry Ford Museum & Greenfield Village, Dearborn, MI (24-B-50). **Page 69**: Colonial Williamsburg Foundation, Williamsburg, VA. **Page 70**: America Hurrah, NYC. **Page 71**: courtesy of Kelter-Malcé, NYC/photo by Schecter Lee. **Pages 72, 73**: America Hurrah, NYC. **Pages 74-75**: sewing boxes, leather needlebook, tartanware drum case, Mauchline wooden cases (on sewing box), Mauchline wooden bottle case, burled acorn case, brass thimbles, stone needle pusher—Tender Buttons, NYC; horseshoe case, silver walnut case, folk-art rabbit case, plastic cases, star case and gold thimble, thimble rings, glass thimbles, cloisonné thimbles, advertising thimbles, leather thimble, silver thimbles, delft thimble—Primose Lane, Manhasset, NY/photo by Stephen Donelian. **Pages 76-82**: (all) Shelburne Museum, Inc., Shelburne, VT/photos by Ken Burris. **Page 83**: collection of the Museum of American Folk Art, NYC, gift of the Trustees of the Museum of American Folk Art (1979.7.1). **Page 84**: America Hurrah, NYC. **Page 85**: Thos. K. Woodard American Antiques & Quilts, NYC. **Page 86**: Shelburne Museum, Inc., Shelburne, VT/photo by Ken Burris. **Page 87**: © Chun Y. Lai/Esto. **Page 88**: Shelburne Museum, Inc., Shelburne, VT/photo by Ken Burris. **Page 89**: America Hurrah, NYC/ photo by Steven Mays. **Pages 90-91**: (background quilt) America Hurrah, NYC; (top row, left to right) collection of Sandra Mitchell; Robert Cargo Folk Art Gallery, Tuscaloosa, AL; America Hurrah, NYC; (bottom row, left) America Hurrah, NYC; (bottom row, right) The Quilt Digest Press, San Francisco, CA, first published in *The Quilt Digest 2*. **Page 92**: Shelburne Museum, Inc., Shelburne, VT/photo by Ken Burris. **Page 94**: courtesy of the Pilgrim Society, Plymouth, MA. **Page 95**: (top) courtesy of the Henry Francis du Pont Winterthur Museum, Winterthur, DE; (bottom) the Allentown Art Museum, Allentown, PA, gift of the Reverend and Mrs. Van S. Merle-Smith, Jr. **Page 96**: (top) collection of Frank and Barbara Pollack; (bottom) courtesy of Harold and Judith Weissman/photo by Schecter Lee. **Page 97**: Shelburne Museum, Inc., Shelburne, VT/photo by Ken Burris. **Page 98**: (top) Shelburne Museum, Inc., Shelburne, VT; (bottom) America Hurrah, NYC. **Page 99**: (top) courtesy of Jeannine Dobbs/photo by Schecter Lee; (bottom) collection of Gail van der Hoof and Jonathan Holstein/photo courtesy of Thos. K. Woodard American Antiques & Quilts, NYC. **Page 100**: Seaver Center for Western History Research, Natural History Museum of Los Angeles County, Los Angeles, CA. **Page 101**: (top) Eleanor and Stephen Score/ photo courtesy of Thos. K. Woodard American Antiques & Quilts, NYC; (bottom) Thos. K. Woodard American Antiques & Quilts, NYC. **Pages 102, 103**: (all) collection of Rosalind and Edwin Miller/photo by Steven Mays. **Pages 104, 105**: (all) Pocumtuck Valley Memorial Association, Memorial Hall Museum, Deerfield, MA. **Page 106**: America Hurrah, NYC. **Page 108**: private collection. **Page 109**: (both) America Hurrah, NYC. **Page 110**: (top) collection of Courcier and Wilkins, photo courtesy of America Hurrah, NYC; (bottom) New York State Historical Association, Cooperstown, NY. **Page 111**: (top) Old Sturbridge Village, Sturbridge, MA/photo by Henry E. Peach; (bottom) Shelburne Museum, Inc., Shelburne, VT/photo by Ken Burris. **Page 112**: (both) private collection. **Page 114**: America Hurrah, NYC. **Page 115**: Shelburne Museum, Inc., Shelburne, VT/photo by Ken Burris. **Page 116**: (top) collection of Barbara Johnson; (bottom) America Hurrah, NYC. **Page 117**: (both) America Hurrah, NYC. **Page 118**: (both) America Hurrah, NYC. **Page 119**: (top) Shaker Village of Pleasant Hill, Harrodsburg, KY; (bottom) America Hurrah, NYC. **Page 120**: (top) America Hurrah, NYC; (bottom) courtesy of David A. Schorsch, Inc., NYC. **Pages 121-124**: (all) collection of Barbara Johnson. **Page 125**: (top) collection of Barbara Johnson; (bottom) Shelburne Museum, Inc., Shelburne, VT/photo by Ken Burris. **Page 126**: (both) © Esto. **Page 127**: (top) America Hurrah, NYC; (bottom) collection of Barbara Johnson/photo by Schecter Lee. **Page 128**: (both) collection of Barbara Johnson. **Page 129**: (top) America Hurrah, NYC; (bottom) collection of Dr. and Mrs. Donald M. Herr/photo © 1977 by Anita Schorsch, from her book *Pastoral Dreams* published by Main Street Press, Universe Books. **Page 130**: (left) America Hurrah, NYC; (right) collection of Barbara Johnson. **Page 131**: (top) collection of Barbara Johnson; (bottom) America Hurrah, NYC. **Page 132**: from the collections of Henry Ford Museum & Greenfield Village, Dearborn, MI (24-G-213). **Page 133**: (top) collection of Rosalind and Edwin Miller; (bottom) The Metropolitan Museum of Art, NYC, Sansbury-Mills Fund, 1961 (61.47.1). **Pages 134-135**: (portrait) from the collections of Henry Ford Museum & Greenfield Village, Dearborn, MI (B42301); (top row, left, and bottom row, left) from the *Descriptive Catalogue of E. S. Frost & Co.'s Hooked Rug Patterns,* © 1970 by The Edison Institute, Dearborn, MI; (top row, right, and second row, both) from the collections of Henry Ford Museum & Greenfield Village, Dearborn, MI (D8004); (third row, left) courtesy of The Winterthur Library, Printed Book and Periodical Collection, Winterthur, DE; (third row, right) private collection/photo by Bradley Olman; (bottom row, right) collection of Barbara Johnson. **Page 136**: (top) private collection; (bottom) private collection/photo by George Ross. **Page 137**: collection of Susan and Richard Berman/photo by Steven Mays. **Page 138**: (top) Shelburne Museum, Inc., Shelburne, VT/photo by Ken Burris; (bottom) © Chun Y. Lai/Esto. **Page 139**: Shelburne Museum, Inc., Shelburne, VT/photo by Ken Burris. **Page 140**: photo by Paul Rocheleau. **Page 141**: (top) courtesy of Kelter-Malcé, NYC/photo by Schecter Lee; (bottom) reprinted by permission of Good Books, Intercourse, PA. **Pages 142, 143**: The Metropolitan Museum of Art, NYC, gift of Katherine Keyes, in memory of her father, Homer Eaton Keyes, 1938 (38.157). **Pages 144-153**: textile and needlework collection of June and Alan Goodrich, Antiques-Folk Art, Erwinna, PA/photos by George Ross. **Pages 154-157**: needlework collection of Carol and Stephen Huber, East Lyme, CT/photos by George Ross. **Pages 158-165**: needlework collection of Thos. K. Woodard American Antiques & Quilts, NYC/photos by George Ross. **Pages 166, 167**: illustrations by Ray Skibinski.

Index

Acknowledgments

Our thanks to Linda Baumgarten of the Colonial Williamsburg Foundation, Susan and Richard Berman, Alberta Brandt of the Henry Francis du Pont Winterthur Museum, Kathy Francis of the Museum of American Textile History, Riki Gail, Cora Ginsburg, Merle Good of Good Books, June and Alan Goodrich, Blanche Greenstein, Catherine H. Grosfils of the Colonial Williamsburg Foundation, Titi Halle, Dr. and Mrs. Donald M. Herr, Carol and Stephen Huber, Susan and Stephen Hunkins, Barbara Johnson, Kate and Joel Kopp, Rosalind and Edwin Miller, Celia Oliver of Shelburne Museum, Inc., David Pottinger, Robert Shaw of Shelburne Museum, Inc., Laurie Suber of the Colonial Williamsburg Foundation, Susan Swan of the Henry Francis du Pont Winterthur Museum, Anne Watkins of the Abby Aldrich Rockefeller Folk Art Center, and Thomas K. Woodard for their help on this book.

First printing
Published simultaneously in Canada
School and library distribution by Silver Burdett Company,
Morristown, New Jersey

TIME-LIFE is a trademark of Time Incorporated U.S.A.

Production by Giga Communications, Inc.
Printed in U.S.A.

Library of Congress Cataloging-in-Publication Data

The Needle arts
p.   cm. — (American country)
Includes index.
ISBN 0-8094-6841-7 — ISBN 0-8094-6842-5 (lib. bdg.)
1. Needlework—United States.
2. Decorative arts, Early American.
I. Time-Life Books.   II. Series.
NK8803.5.N44   1990   746'.0974—dc20   90-11002
CIP

American Country was created by Rebus, Inc., and published by Time-Life Books.

REBUS, INC.

Publisher: RODNEY FRIEDMAN • Editor: MARYA DALRYMPLE
Executive Editor: RACHEL D. CARLEY • Managing Editor: BRENDA SAVARD • Consulting Editor: CHARLES L. MEE, JR.
Copy Editor: ALEXA RIPLEY BARRE
Writers: JUDITH CRESSY, ROSEMARY G. RENNICKE • Freelance Writer: JOE L. ROSSON
Design Editors: NANCY MERNIT, CATHRYN SCHWING
Test Kitchen Director: GRACE YOUNG • Editor, The Country Letter: BONNIE J. SLOTNICK
Contributing Editors: LEE CUTRONE, ANNE MOFFAT, CATHERINE RITZINGER
Indexer: MARILYN FLAIG

Art Director: JUDITH HENRY • Associate Art Director: SARA REYNOLDS
Designers: AMY BERNIKER, TIMOTHY JEFFS
Photographer: STEVEN MAYS • Photo Editor: SUE ISRAEL
Photo Assistant: ROB WHITCOMB • Freelance Photographers: STEPHEN DONELIAN, GEORGE ROSS
Freelance Photo Stylists: VALORIE FISHER, DEE SHAPIRO • Set Carpenter: MARCOS SORENSEN

Special Consultant for this book: MARGARET VINCENT
Series Consultants: BOB CAHN, HELAINE W. FENDELMAN, LINDA C. FRANKLIN, GLORIA GALE,
KATHLEEN EAGEN JOHNSON, JUNE SPRIGG, CLAIRE WHITCOMB

Time-Life Books Inc. is a wholly owned subsidiary of THE TIME INC. BOOK COMPANY.

President and Chief Executive Officer: KELSO F. SUTTON
President, Time Inc. Books Direct: CHRISTOPHER T. LINEN

TIME-LIFE BOOKS INC.

Editor: GEORGE CONSTABLE
Director of Design: LOUIS KLEIN • Director of Editorial Resources: PHYLLIS K. WISE
Director of Photography and Research: JOHN CONRAD WEISER

President: JOHN M. FAHEY JR.
Senior Vice Presidents: ROBERT M. DeSENA, PAUL R. STEWART, CURTIS G. VIEBRANZ, JOSEPH J. WARD
Vice Presidents: STEPHEN L. BAIR, BONITA L. BOEZEMAN, MARY P. DONOHOE, STEPHEN L. GOLDSTEIN,
ANDREW P. KAPLAN, TREVOR LUNN, SUSAN J. MARUYAMA, ROBERT H. SMITH
New Product Development: TREVOR LUNN, DONIA ANN STEELE
Supervisor of Quality Control: JAMES KING

Publisher: JOSEPH J. WARD

For information about any Time-Life book please call 1-800-621-7026, or write:
Reader Information, Time-Life Customer Service
P.O. Box C-32068, Richmond, Virginia 23261-2068

Time-Life Books Inc. offers a wide range of fine recordings, including a Rock 'n' Roll Era series.
For subscription information, call 1-800-621-7026, or write TIME-LIFE MUSIC,
P.O. Box C-32068, Richmond, Virginia 23261-2068.